# THEN & NOW

# fARMING

## KATIE RODEN

**FRANKLIN WATTS**
LONDON • SYDNEY

An Aladdin Book
© Aladdin Books Ltd
1996

Designed and
produced by
**Aladdin Books Ltd**
28 Percy Street
London W1P 0LD

ISBN 0 7496 2469 8

First published in
Great Britain in 1996
by
**Franklin Watts**
96 Leonard Street
London EC2A 4RH

Consultant
Wullie Findlay is
curator at the Scottish
Agricultural Museum
at Ingliston.

Editor
Jon Richards

Design

**David West**
CHILDREN'S BOOK DESIGN
Designers
Flick Killerby
Edward Simkins

Picture Research
Brooks Krikler
Research

Illustrator
James Field, Stephen
Sweet – Simon Girling
& Associates

Printed in Belgium
All rights reserved

A CIP catalogue entry
for this book is
available from the
British Library

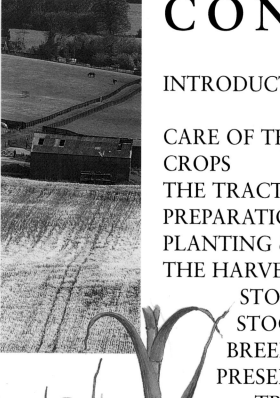

# CONTENTS

# INTRODUCTION

Farming has existed for almost as long as the human race itself. The first farmers experimented with planting seeds, herding and rearing animals and preparing the ground. They knew little about caring for the soil or breeding the best types of animal. Today, scientists strive constantly to produce better livestock and plants, while the conservation of the soil and the Earth's other natural resources is an important issue worldwide. This book describes the origins and development of many of the farming methods that are used around the world.

Farming as we know it faces a future of great change. After thousands of years, and especially after heavy use in the twentieth century, the Earth's resources are becoming exhausted. New farming methods must be found in order to restore and improve them. The latest technology is now being used to develop new techniques, including underwater farming and cultivation in space. But the reason that farming is so important has remained the same throughout history: to meet the world's increasing need for food, clothing, fuel, wood, medicine and a wide range of other vital products.

# CARE OF THE LAND

Early peoples rarely took care of their farmland. They were unaware that soil must be looked after if it is to consistently produce massive amounts of food.

Over the centuries, the world's population has increased, taking up more land to live on. This means that less land is available for farming. As a result, the available land has to be looked after very carefully to grow enough food. Water must be made available through irrigation systems such as ditches. Also, as certain crops take nutrients out of the soil, these nutrients have to be replaced to stop the soil from becoming useless.

### GUARDIANS OF THE SOIL

Many early peoples worshipped gods of agriculture and performed ceremonies to please them and so ensure a good harvest. This carved stone from Mesopotamia (c. 2900 BC, *above*) shows the worship of a grain god.

### FLOODING THE LAND

Some crops, such as rice, need a lot of water to grow. To create a rice paddy (field), channels are dug in the mud *(left)*. The ground is ploughed and flooded, then seedlings are planted.

## WASTE NOT, WANT NOT

One of the oldest, most efficient systems of land irrigation was developed by the ancient Egyptians. Once a year, the River Nile would flood, swamping the dry farmland on its banks. The Egyptians dug deep ditches beside their fields *(below)*. The flood water would flow into these channels. It was stored and used to water the fields when the Nile was low again.

### SURFACE DRAINAGE

This ancient method *(top)* uses ditches which carry excess water away from the soil, so that it does not flood the land. It is used on flat ground, where water cannot flow away, and in areas of high rainfall. Surface drains are useful for types of soil that do not absorb water well, such as clay. But they also get in the way of people and machinery!

## THE ROMANS

*The Roman Empire (753 BC-AD 476) covered many countries, from Africa and Asia to northern Europe. As its armies advanced, they discovered and passed on many farming techniques. Some of these, including crop rotation, are still in use today.*

Crops have been grown on artificial terraces for centuries. Rice was cultivated in this way in Asia over 5,000 years ago, while the Romans built terraces for grapes and olives *(right)*. Wide "steps" are cut into a hillside then planted. Excess water drains down the hill, but the soil is not washed away.

Turnips

Barley

Wheat

Peas

Surface channels

## CROP CIRCLES

Crop rotation, a Roman discovery, was developed in the 1700s when Charles Townshend of Britain introduced 4-field rotation *(left)*. By rotating wheat, peas, barley and turnips, a farmer does not exhaust the soil, as peas and turnips replace nutrients that wheat and barley take out.

Drainage pipes

### SLASH AND BURN
This ancient method of ground preparation is still used in South America, Asia and Africa. The farmer cuts down the trees and plants in a small area of forest, then burns the cuttings *(below)*. The ashes add nutrients to the soil. Crops such as fruit and root vegetables are then planted in the burnt area. Many farmers plant crops that grow at different times of the year. This method ensures a good food supply, but it can be damaging to the forest if practised on too wide a scale.

### SUB-SURFACE DRAINAGE
This method is much more practical than surface drainage. Buried pipes have small holes to let in water, which is carried away for disposal. Many are surrounded by gravel to stop soil from getting in.

# CROPS

Over thousands of years, peoples around the world have discovered which plants are safe to eat, which plants can be grown in certain regions and how to harvest crops successfully. Today, technology has greatly improved the production and increased the quality of crops. The techniques used include combining the best qualities of different plants and developing fertilisers and pesticides. These have given us an amazing variety of fruit, vegetables and other food crops.

**EARLY ALCOHOL**
The cultivation of grapes to make wine dates from at least 5000 BC. Christians spread wine-making methods, many of which are still used today.

**MAIZE GODS**
Maize (corn) was first grown in South America. The crop was so important that it even had its own gods, as shown by this statue *(above)* made by the Mochica people of Peru.

**THE FIRST FARMERS**
In about 9000 BC, people realised that plants grew from seeds and could be cultivated. They began to gather and plant a variety of seeds, to ensure that they had a constant food supply.

*Neolithic sickle*

**PROTECTIVE SYSTEMS**
Care for crops does not end with harvesting. On banana plantations, each bunch is cut down and wrapped carefully to protect it *(right)*.

**CEREALS**
Ancient Egyptian paintings show wheat harvests *(above)*. Cereal farming methods changed little until the invention of the seed drill *(see page 12)*, when crops could be sown more efficiently.

## SWEET CROPS

Cane sugar *(left)* was grown on Pacific islands over 8,000 years ago. Cultivation had spread to China and Europe by AD 636. European settlers planted cane in America and took it to Australia. In 1799, it was discovered that beet also produced sugar. Today, nearly 40% of the world's sugar comes from beet.

6

## A NICE CUP OF TEA

In Chinese legend, tea-drinking was invented by Emperor Shang Yeng in 2737 BC. The first record of tea-drinking in China dates from AD 350. By AD 600, it had become a Japanese custom. Tea was first taken to Europe by Dutch merchants in 1610. Today, there are vast plantations in China, Indonesia, eastern Africa, India and Japan. The best tea comes from the tender leaves at the top of the plant, which are still picked by hand.

### THE POTATO

Potatoes were first grown by the Incas in South America and were taken to Europe in the sixteenth century. Although early potatoes were picked by hand, today's crops are gathered using harvesters. Sweet potatoes, which also came from South America, are grown a lot in tropical countries.

## A FRUITY HISTORY

Using scientific techniques *(see pages 20-21)*, fruit growers can now produce plants that grow without the care they needed during the Middle Ages *(above)*. For example, until recently the British cherry crop was devastated by birds, which could easily eat the fruit growing in tall, unprotected trees. In the last few years, growers have developed a smaller tree which can be covered to protect the fruit.

### THE COCONUT

*This is probably one of the world's most versatile plants! The trees provide: wood for building; leaves which can be used for roofing or hats; and sap for sugar, vinegar and alcohol. The flesh and milk of the nut are nutritious foods.*

### THE TERRIBLE CONSEQUENCE

After the sixteenth century, Europeans transported slaves from Africa to work on their farms. Life for the slaves on the plantations was appalling *(right)*. The workers were chained and beaten, and had little food or water.

# THE TRACTOR

The tractor is one of the most important inventions in the history of farming, and today there are about 26 million in use around the world. The earliest tractors were powered by steam. They were extremely powerful, but awkward to drive.

Today, tractors vary in size and shape, from massive monsters, powered by turbo-diesel engines, to lighter, multi-purpose models. Around the farm, the tractor performs two roles: pulling loads efficiently and powering other equipment.

**STRONG AS AN OX**
The word "tractor" comes from "traction" (pulling) and it is this feature which makes the vehicle so important. It has more strength than the oxen or horses used in traditional farming methods *(above)*, and it can work steadily without resting.

## THE AGE OF STEAM

Built in the mid-nineteenth century, steam-powered machines were known as "traction engines" *(right)*. These engines were used to power a number of machines, including threshers. The traction engine would pull the thresher into the fields and power it while it threshed the crop.

*1870s*

**THE STEAM ENGINE**
Steam engines *(left)* were operated by the expansion of steam, which pushed pistons up and down. Oil, wood or coal was burnt in a furnace to heat water in a boiler, which then produced the steam.

**PULLING POWER**
Tractors can pull an amazing array of equipment *(below)*, such as ploughs and harrows. They can also be used to power mowing machines and spray pumps.

**LIGHTNESS OR STRENGTH?**
The early petrol tractors *(right)* were small and light. However, they were not really powerful enough to pull the large machinery found around today's farms.

# PETROL POWER

In the 1890s, the first efficient petrol engines, built into the tractor frame were introduced in the USA. The all-purpose tractor *(left)* was invented in the 1920s. This could power all kinds of equipment and quickly replaced steam engines and animals on almost all US farms, then around the world. Modern tractors are run using diesel engines rather than petrol ones, as they are more efficient.

*HARRY FERGUSON (1884-1960) Ferguson was an Irish engineer. In 1909, he built a plane and became the first person in Ireland to fly. But he is most famous for the Ferguson farm tractor, with hydraulic linkage (worked by water) which gave more control and stability. This helped to speed up the mechanisation of farming worldwide.*

**TRACTOR FEATURES**
The most important features of a modern tractor are those which allow it to pull and power other equipment. These include: the **drawbar,** to which machinery is attached; the **power take-off** which powers the equipment pulled by the tractor; and the **hydraulic system** which can alter the position of equipment attached to the tractor.

**THE MANUFACTURERS**
The first tractor-making companies manufactured only one type or size of vehicle, such as this "Saunderson Tractor" *(left)*. Industrial technology now allows manufacturers to make a range of tractors, designed to suit different farming needs *(below)*.

*Renault 180-94 TZ multishift tractor*

**SHAPES AND SIZES**
The largest farm tractors are huge four-wheel drive machines that weigh up to 7.5 tonnes *(left)*. Most tractors are two-wheel drive and can weigh as little as 1.4 tonnes.

# PREPARATION

Thousands of years ago, people realised that plants grow better in loose soil, which lets in more air and water than undisturbed ground. They began to turn the earth over with sticks, bones and rocks.

About 8,000 years ago, there was a breakthrough – the invention of the *ard*, a hand-pulled plough made from a large, forked branch. One prong was sharpened then charred in a fire to make it harder. As this hardened point was pulled through the soil it made a furrow. *Ards* are still used in some countries today.

### FEEDING THE GROUND
Before the invention of the plough, early peoples used sticks to make holes for air and water *(above)*.

### BEASTS OF BURDEN
By 3000 BC, Egyptian and Mesopotamian farmers used oxen to pull ploughs *(top)*, so increasing the areas which could be planted. Roman explorers took this method back to Europe.

### THE HORSE ARRIVES
Oxen *(below)* were gradually replaced by horses for ploughing. By the AD 900s, the horse-drawn plough was common in many parts of the world. At the start of the Industrial Revolution, in about 1765, James Small of Britain designed and made the first cast-iron plough.

*Mouldboard ploughs* (left) *have been used since the Middle Ages, as they are the most versatile type.*

## INNOVATIONS
Small's plough was redesigned in the USA in 1830 by James Oliver. He divided the plough into parts which could be mass-produced and bought individually. Today, many farms use a cultivator instead of a plough to aerate (put air into) the soil. Instead of turning the soil over, this piece of equipment, pulled behind a tractor, uses a series of long spikes which dig deep into the ground.

### POWER PLOUGHING
By the early nineteenth century, steam-powered ploughs were being developed. Each plough was fixed by ropes to two steam engines *(right)*.

One engine would pull the plough across the field. When it reached the first engine, the plough was moved to the site of the next furrow. The second engine would then pull the plough back.

JOHN DEERE (1804-86)
*Deere, a US blacksmith, designed various ploughs with a partner. But he won fame in 1840 when he invented the cast-steel plough, which made it easier to turn heavy soil. He also made a "sulky" plough with wheels and a seat.*

DEERE'S PLOUGH

TYPES OF PLOUGH
Because soils vary, different designs of cutting tools are needed on ploughs.
The main cutting tools are: **mouldboard** – the most widely used type, which buries waste matter from old crops; **disc** – for sticky or tough soil; **rotary** – mixes old crop material with the soil; **drill** – lifts the soil without turning it.

*This tractor (right) is pulling a plough which is fitted with a mouldboard cutting tool. This buries old crop remains in the soil as it ploughs the field.*

# MODERN PLOUGHING

Both traditional and modern methods are used to plough fields today. Farmers in developing countries still use walking ploughs, pulled by animals, as machinery is expensive. Most farmers in developed countries use a tractor plough made from steel or iron *(left)* or a cultivator, which requires an extremely powerful tractor to pull it.

11

# PLANTING & GROWING

**THE INGENIOUS INCAS**
Most Inca people of South America lived in rural, agricultural communities and so developed highly efficient farming methods. They used foot-ploughs tipped with hard wood or bronze to turn the soil, and digging sticks to help their planting *(above)*.

Until the early eighteenth century, sowing seeds was done by hand. But hand-sowing was not very precise. Precious seeds were thrown out at random by the sower and some could easily land on bad ground. In the late 1800s, a hand-held sowing machine, or "seed fiddle", was invented. This allowed the sower to spread seeds more accurately and easily. Today, tractor-pulled seed drills are used.

**DIBBLE AWAY!**
Digging sticks, or "dibblers" *(above)*, were pushed into the ground to make a single hole. A seed could then be planted, making sowing more accurate and efficient.

## NO MORE BACKACHE!

A revolution in sowing came in 1701, when an English farmer, Jethro Tull, invented the seed drill *(above)* – the first farm machine with moving parts. The drill had a "coulter" (cutter) to carve a "drill" (furrow) in the soil. The grain was stored in a seed box and pushed out by a rotating brush. It fell into a hole, down a funnel and into the furrow. The drill operator would tread soil into the furrow to bury the grain. The size of the hole could be altered, to sow different varieties of seed.

RESTRICTED

LOST HILLS FLYING SERVICE, INC.

AG WAGON

N9335R

## INTENSIVE GROWTH

As global demand for food has increased, technology has been used to improve production. Today, huge commercial greenhouses, some of them solar powered, are used to grow crops out of season, such as tomatoes, cucumbers and even flowers. Many have computer controls to alter the heat, soil, fertiliser and light, the amount of water given to the plants and the humidity of the air.

### PAUL HERMANN MÜLLER (1899-1965)

*Müller, a Swiss chemist, discovered the insecticide properties of the chemical DDT in 1939. He won a Nobel Prize in 1948. But DDT is now banned in many places.*

### WHAT A PEST!

The late 1800s and early 1900s saw the development of chemicals to control diseases and pests, such as weevils *(left)*. But in the 1950s, many, including DDT, were found to harm the environment. Today, alternatives are being developed.

### SWARM!

The locust is feared in Africa and the Middle East. Locusts have huge appetites – a single insect will eat its own weight in food every day. If a large number crowd together, they form a swarm of up to 1,000 million insects. Wherever they settle, they eat – a swarm can eat 20,000 tonnes of plants in a day, making locusts disastrous for crop farmers.

## FERTILE SOIL

Fertilisers have been used for thousands of years. At first, they came from natural sources, such as manure. By the 1900s, botanists knew that plants needed certain chemicals to thrive, and so made artificial fertilisers containing them. Other plants can be used to replace nutrients – beans and peas are grown with rubber trees to feed the soil.

### CROP SPRAYING

Crop-spraying planes and helicopters are used on large farms to scatter pesticide or fertilisers. A farmer can quickly deliver a precise amount of chemicals over a very wide area in a short space of time.

*Clappers*

### STRAW PEOPLE

Scarecrows *(right)*, date from the eighteenth century. Until then, birds were kept off growing crops by children, often standing alone in the fields, who shouted at the birds and used clappers *(above)* or rattles. Today, mechanical bird scarers are used. These emit high-pitched noises and the sound of gunshots.

13

# THE HARVEST

Traditionally, crops were harvested by hand *(left)*, either by picking them from trees and bushes or by cutting them with scythes *(right)*. This is still the case for some crops, such as tea, grapes and rice. However, massive combine harvesters usually do all the jobs needed to gather a variety of plants. They can do the work of hundreds of people in a fraction of the time and in all conditions.

### ANCIENT HARVESTS
Images of the harvest are found among all ancient civilisations. They were often put in places of worship, as offerings to the gods in return for a good crop the next year. Many religions still hold harvest ceremonies.

*Bronze Age sickle*

### CUTTING THE CORN
Scythes and sickles have been used since ancient times. The scythe dates at least from the Roman era and was used to cut crops in a single, strong stroke. The sickle *(above)*, a smaller, lighter version, has been used since prehistoric times. Sickles are still used widely today, despite the development of machinery, because they are cheap to make and easy to use.

*Iron Age sickle*

*Handle*

*Grassnail*

### THE SCYTHE
This consists of a long, straight handle made of wood with a metal blade, supported by a metal *grassnail*. Originally, scythes were sharpened with a *straik (below)* – a piece of pitted wood smeared with mutton fat and soft or stony sand, depending on the sharpness needed.

*Straik*

### THRESHING
Threshing (separating) grains from stalks and winnowing (blowing) the husks from the grains were done by hand until 1780, when Andrew Mieckle of Scotland built the first threshing machine. Early threshers were powered by horse, which walked on a treadmill *(right)*. Horse power was replaced in the mid-1800s by steam engines.

### FARMING... ON A MASSIVE SCALE!
China grows the most crops in the world – about 19% of the Earth's total production. This is followed by the USA with about 14%, then by Russia.

The most efficient harvest ever gathered was collected by an agricultural team in Britain. With a single combine harvester, they gathered 358 tonnes of wheat in only eight hours in August 1990!

1

14

## PATRICK BELL (1799-1869)

*Bell, a Scottish minister, invented a mechanical reaper in 1827, but it did not catch on quickly. In 1834, Cyrus McCormick of the USA produced a similar machine which was adapted into a combined reaper and binder.*

# MULTI-PURPOSE MACHINES

In the early 1900s, work began on a combined reaper and thresher. It had an engine which worked the moving parts *(above)*. Today, combines come in many sizes, to suit different crops and sizes of field. They have special attachments to harvest crops other than cereals, such as soybeans and cotton. Some are designed to harvest unusual crops like trees or potatoes. Most are self-propelled, although the smallest may be pulled by tractors.

HOW THE COMBINE WORKS
1. A cutting bar cuts the stalks with rotating paddles.
2. The stalks fall onto a platform and are carried by a feeder to a threshing drum. A revolving cylinder separates the grain from the stalks, then the stalks are discarded and used for straw.
3. The grain passes through sieves and the husks are blown away by a fan.
4. The grain is fed into a tank. From here it is poured into lorries and taken away for storage.

# STOCK FARMS

Prehistoric peoples lived as hunter-gatherers – hunting animals and collecting plants and berries for food. Certain people still practise this lifestyle in the more remote parts of the world. However, about 9,000 years ago, the herding and breeding of animals such as sheep and cattle were developed in the Middle East. These provided people with a regular supply of milk, eggs, wool and meat.

Today, farmers breed an amazing array of animals to keep pace with the increase in demand for food. These range from dairy cattle, fish and pigs to llamas, ostriches and even crocodiles.

**STONE AGE HERDERS**
This 5,000-year-old rock painting *(above)*, in the Sahara Desert of Africa, shows cattle herding. At that time, parts of the Sahara were grassland. The herders may have travelled up to 2,500 km (1,500 miles) in search of fodder.

**THE FIRST COWBOYS**
By 1500 BC, herders were using horses and camels to help control their animals. Nomadic farmers like Arab warrior-herders *(above)* could now travel even further. Modern herders are more likely to use motorbikes!

## NOMADIC HERDING

This was the original method of stock farming. Nomadic herders would allow small herds of animals like goats or cattle to wander freely as they searched for fresh pastures. This ensured that the herd was always well fed and the farmer had a constant supply of meat. Nomadic herding still occurs. For example, the Sami of Lapland travel with herds of reindeer.

*Sumerian cattle herders, c. 3000 BC*

*Egyptian goose farmers*

## POULTRY

Chickens were tamed in prehistoric times and were bred in China over 3,000 years ago. Turkeys came from Mexico and were taken by explorers back to Europe via Turkey. Geese were kept in Egypt over 4,000 years ago *(above)* and were later reared by the Greeks and Romans.

## A PIGGY HISTORY

Wild pigs lived in Europe up to 6 million years ago. During the Stone Age, early peoples began to tame and breed them. They were taken to North and South America in the 1500s and to Australia and New Zealand in the eighteenth century.

## RANCHING

In places with poorer-quality grazing, such as Australia, New Zealand, the southern USA and South America, stock farms may be spread over vast areas, known as ranches. The animals can wander freely in search of food. They are rounded up *(below)* only when it is time for shearing or dipping *(see pages 18-19)* or if they are to be sold.

*ELIZABETH MACARTHUR (1766-1850) MacArthur emigrated from England to Australia in 1789. She introduced merino sheep to the country and bred them to produce the finest possible wool. This formed the basis of the Australian wool trade, which today is one of the country's most profitable industries.*

ELIZABETH MACARTHUR'S SHEEP

*Holstein-Friesian cattle*

## THE HISTORICAL COW

For thousands of years, water buffalo have been used in Asia for ploughing and other heavy tasks. The Romans were the first to breed cattle selectively. In 100 BC, the first specialised dairy cow – the Holstein-Friesian *(above)* – was introduced. This type of breeding continued throughout the Middle Ages. Nowadays, farmers keep a wide variety of cattle for both their meat and their milk. These include Jersey, Brahman and Hereford cattle.

## FARMS AS FAR AS THE EYE CAN SEE

Australia, with its enormous tracts of land, has the largest stock farms in the world. The country's biggest cattle ranch, at Anna Creek, covers an amazing 30,000 square kilometres (11,600 square miles). The world's largest sheep ranch, in South Australia, covers 10,567 square kilometres (4,080 square miles).

# STOCK METHODS

Animal farming has changed a great deal in the last 10,000 years. New techniques in the treatment of animals have improved the production of meat, milk, eggs and wool – some cows can now produce over 6,000 litres (10,500 pints) of milk a year! Animals can be protected from illness, allowing them to live longer. However, some modern methods of animal rearing are causing concern.

## HANDY MILKING
Milking was first done by hand *(below)*, and is still done this way in parts of the world. In ancient Babylon, India and Egypt, each family kept a cow to provide milk.

## THE MILKING MACHINE

It is not quite clear when the milking machine was invented, as many designs were proposed over the years. In 1878, Anna Baldwin, a US farmer, invented a machine that obtained milk by suction. But milking machines only became successful after 1898, when J. Wallis from Scotland invented the pulsator. This mimicked the sucking action of the calf, and is still used today.

**POOR COWS!** Early machines *(above, 1862)* were not invented with much concern for the cow! The udders were often squeezed extremely hard in order to force out the milk.

*Pulsator*

*LOUIS PASTEUR (1822-95) Pasteur, a French scientist, discovered that diseases are spread by bacteria. He showed that cows and sheep could be protected from anthrax by being injected with some of the bacteria. By keeping animals alive longer, his work revolutionised farming.*

**MAKING MILK**
Today's milking parlours *(above)* are kept very clean. After the cow has been milked, the "raw milk" must be treated to remove any harmful bacteria. Once this is done, the milk can be turned into a variety of products, such as yoghurt and butter.

18

## A CONTROVERSIAL ISSUE

The growth of intensive farming has caused great debate. Conditions in fattening houses and battery farms are often poor and cramped. They are not good for the physical and mental health of the animals or for the quality of their produce.

## DINNER TIME

Special feeds can increase milk and meat production. The amount given to each animal is controlled. Some farms have links to computers at agricultural colleges, which tell them what quantities to use.

## ANIMAL AILMENTS

There are many types of disease, but the most common are mastitis, brucellosis, foot and mouth, tsetse fly and liver rot. The new disease of BSE, caught from contaminated cattle feed, is spreading in Britain. Parasites are usually controlled by dipping animals in insecticide.

## RAWHIDE!

A year on a cattle ranch begins in autumn, when some of the cattle are sold. Preparation for winter involves buying food which is given to the herd if it snows. Calves are born in spring and are rounded up and branded. They are grazed through the summer.

# INTENSIVE FARMING

This method was developed in the twentieth century in response to an increasing demand for food. As many animals as possible are reared in the space available. Pigs are raised in fattening houses *(left)*, while battery farms contain thousands of chickens *(above left)*. Both are given special food to improve production. Opponents prefer free-range farming *(above right)*, in which animals are kept in more open spaces.

# SHEEP MANAGEMENT

Originally found wild in the mountains of central Asia, sheep have been carefully bred over the centuries. Today, there are over 800 breeds. The sheep are sheared each year to obtain their wool, and are dipped regularly in insecticide to kill parasites that may live in the fleece. Traditionally, sheep were sheared using hand shears. Today's shearers use electric clippers. A good shearer, like those working on the Australian sheep stations *(right)*, can shear over 200 sheep in a single day.

# BREEDING

Since farming began, people have looked for ways of breeding better animals and plants, to improve their yield and to produce varieties suited to specific purposes. In 1700, Robert Bakewell of Britain invented a method of improving the quality of livestock by breeding animals with desirable characteristics. This has led to a huge variety of animals, each bred for specific needs – for example, Charolais cattle are reared only for their meat.

New varieties of plants are being developed all the time: to provide more or better-quality food for humans and animals; to grow faster; to be disease-resistant; or to survive in harsh climates.

**RIDING POWER**
Horses have been selectively bred for centuries. Arab horses *(above)* were swift and strong. They were taken to Europe after AD 900 and used to breed high-quality horses. Arabs are still valuable today.

**BREEDING TECHNIQUES**
A cross-breed is produced by the mating of animals from different breeds, such as two types of cow *(left)*. Pure-breeding is the mating of the best animals from the same breed.

## ARTIFICIAL INSEMINATION

This technique, developed in the mid-twentieth century, has made selective breeding easier, as the animals do not have to meet. The farmer can control when the cow is ready to become pregnant. When this happens, the farmer buys bull's semen (the fluid which contains sperm). This semen is placed inside the cow, where the sperm fertilises the egg. Using artificial insemination, one bull can be mated to more than 3,000 cows every year.

**A LIVESTOCK LEGEND**
By far the heaviest cattle weight ever recorded was that of Mount Katahdin, a Durham-Holstein cross, in Maine, USA. His weight rose to 2,267 kg (5,000 lb)! In comparison, an average bull weighs about 900 kg (1,980 lb).

**A PERFECT COW?**
The Aberdeen Angus *(above)* has been specially bred for the quality of its meat. It can also adapt to a variety of climates.

### TIME STANDS STILL
These tomatoes and barley (left) have been developed with genes that delay the ripening process. This means that they can be transported over long distances and stay fresh. It also increases the time that they can be displayed in shops.

### GREGOR MENDEL (1822-84)
*Mendel was a monk with an interest in botany. He found that the genes of an organism (its basic features) are inherited by each generation and can be altered by selective breeding. His work formed the basis of modern genetics.*

GREGOR MENDEL

## USES OF SCIENCE
By the 1960s, the science of genetics was firmly established and was producing animals (including fish, *left*) and crops with much higher yields. For example, average maize yields in the USA increased from 69 bushels per hectare in the 1920s to 292 bushels per hectare in the 1980s.

### THE TECHNIQUE
To alter the cells of an organism, two genes with the desired characteristics are split and combined to produce a new gene. This is placed into a cell, which multiplies to form a new organism. Each of its cells contains the altered genetic information.

### STRAWBERRY FIELDS FOREVER
The juicy strawberries of today are very different to their ancestors! Small, wild strawberries *(above left)* were first cultivated by the Romans. It was not until the eighteenth century that they were combined with another variety from Chile. This produced the larger variety that we eat today.

## SUPER PLANTS!
Genetic techniques have produced a wide range of "super plants". Grafting (joining parts of two plants to make one plant) can also determine a plant's characteristics. For example, it can produce seedless fruits, such as grapes, and trees that can bear more than one type of apple. Scientists have also developed bacteria with altered genes, which act as pesticides when they are placed on crops.

# PRESERVATION & TRANSPORT

For centuries, food producers and farmers have faced a major problem – how to transport produce while keeping it as fresh as when it was gathered. And this continues to be a problem, especially as large amounts of food are shipped worldwide. Prehistoric peoples dried food by laying it out in the sun *(below)* and later with fire. In winter, it was put outside to be preserved by the ice and wind. Today, some food, such as bacon *(right)*, is coated with chemicals to mimic the effect of smoking *(see below)*.

### SALTY STORY
Salting has been used for thousands of years. Produce is dried by the salt and so does not go off. Fresh food was put in barrels of salt for sea journeys. Later, chemicals were added to the salt. Salt curing is still carried out, often on an industrial scale.

## A CHILLY STORY
In colder countries, people built ice houses or cellars in their homes, in which food could be preserved by the cold. It was not until 1925 that Clarence Birdseye, a US businessman, invented a method of freezing foods in small quantities that were easy to sell and transport. Modern electric freezers can freeze food quickly and keep it fresh for a long time.

### SMOKING
Ancient peoples preserved meat or fish by smoking it over fires. Different types of wood produced different smoke, which altered the taste of the meat. Smoked meat and fish is still a delicacy.

### CAN IT!
In the 1700s, meat was sealed into glass jars and heated, making it edible for several weeks. This was the basis of modern canning.

*Tin cans, 1835*

### DRYING METHODS
There are various drying techniques: **sun** – food is placed in the sun *(right)*; **freeze** – with dry ice; **tray** – with hot air; **spray** – with air and liquid; **pulse-combustion** – with sound and heat waves.

22

***CLARENCE BIRDSEYE***
***(1886-1956)*** *Birdseye, from the USA, is best remembered for his development of packaged frozen food, and for his companies General Seafoods and Birdseye Frosted Foods. But he was also the inventor of more than 300 other objects, including infra-red heat lamps.*

## THE TRANSPORT DEBATE

The live transport of animals is the best way to ensure the freshness of the meat on arrival, but the methods used have caused great controversy. Animals are often carried in overcrowded lorries, without enough air, water or rest, especially in countries with few regulations.

INTO THE NUCLEAR AGE
The newest development in the preservation of food is the use of gamma rays (a type of radiation similar to X-rays, *left*). The rays destroy the bacteria that contribute to the ripening of produce such as potatoes and other fruit and vegetables. This ripening of the food eventually leads to it going bad.

The destruction of the bacteria slows down the ripening process and allows the produce to be shipped over long distances without rotting before arrival. Gamma radiation is effective, but the risks it might pose to human health are still unknown.

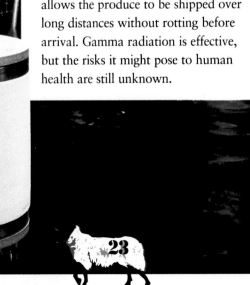

23

# ARE THEY FARMS?

*Silk worms*

As global demand for food and other goods has increased, people have had to turn to new farming methods – from breeding unusual animals, such as crocodiles, for alternative sources of meat, to growing trees and other plants for fuel. For example, huge regions of Brazil have been given over to grow sugar plants, which may be turned into alcohol then used to run cars.

"Wind farms" consist of thousands of wind turbines which convert the power of the wind into electricity, saving the Earth's precious fossil fuel resources.

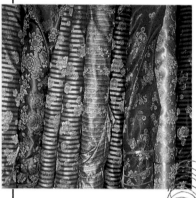

**A CLOSELY GUARDED SECRET**
In Chinese legend, silk was discovered in 2700 BC and was kept secret for 2,000 years. Making silk has not changed much since then. Even in the biggest farms, the cocoons of the larvae *(top left)* are unwrapped by hand to get fine strands of silk.

**LLAMA FARMING**
Llamas, from South America, are wool-bearers that can live in almost any conditions. Llama farming is now a big business.

**HEADS IN THE SAND**
In the late 1800s, ostrich plumes became fashionable accessories in Europe *(left)*. As a result the species was almost wiped out. Ostrich farms soon sprang up in northern and southern Africa, the USA, southern Europe and Australia. By 1918, however, fashions had changed and the plumes were no longer wanted. Ostriches continue to be farmed for eggs, leather and meat.

**RAPE SEED**
Rape, a flowering herb, is farmed in Europe, New Zealand and Asia. It is becoming an important crop because its seeds produce oil. This oil can be used for cooking and to make soap and fuel. It is also used to make cheap feed for livestock.

24

## RUBBER
Native North Americans tapped wild rubber trees for latex to make toys and shoes. Rubber cultivation developed in the 1700s. When the car was invented, worldwide demand for rubber increased. Latex is still tapped by hand.

## A FISHY TALE
Aquaculture (fish farming) has been practised in China for at least 4,000 years, and China still produces the most fish. Today, aquaculture is a good alternative to the overfishing of the seas. All sorts of sea plants and creatures are farmed: **molluscs** such as oysters for food; **seaweeds** for food, fertiliser and animal fodder; **crustaceans** such as lobsters for food; **fish**, both freshwater and marine, such as salmon, for food and natural oils.

### A STING IN THE TAIL
Honey has been used as food since the Stone Age, when early peoples took it from the nests of wild bees. Today, bees are used on the Great Plains of the USA to increase the amount of plants for cattle fodder. Huge mobile hives tour the country. At certain places, the trucks are opened and the bees fly out to feed on the plants, carrying pollen and so fertilising them.

### INSECTS
*In many areas, insects are used as food and some are seen as delicacies, such as the honey-ant of Australia (right). Insects are cheap and nutritious, yet to some people the idea of eating them is revolting. But farming them might be one way to increase the world's food supplies.*

## COTTON
Cotton was first cultivated by the Persians about 5,000 years ago. It was taken to Europe by Alexander the Great's army in the fourth century BC, and spread around the world. In 1793, Eli Whitney of the USA invented the cotton gin *(right)*. This removed seeds, saving hours of labour. Today, there is a wide variety of cotton-picking equipment *(left)*, but it is still harvested by hand in places such as India and Thailand.

25

# PROTECTING THE EARTH

The twentieth century has seen a vast increase in the use of the world's limited natural resources. Without careful management they will soon become exhausted.

Over-fishing has led to a lack of fish stocks in the oceans, and land that has been used for agriculture for thousands of years is now becoming infertile. The deserts are increasing in size, as millions of trees are cut down and more animals are grazed on the land.

Yet more food is needed to feed the increasing population of the world.

**ANCIENT IRRIGATION**
The *shaduf (above)*, used in ancient Egypt, was one of the earliest irrigation tools. Traditional methods of cultivation are being turned to again, in an effort to stop over-farming.

## THE DYING SEAS

The twentieth-century fishing industry operates on a vast scale, catching and processing millions of fish every year. But this means that in many marine waters, such as the northern Atlantic Ocean, fish stocks have been greatly reduced. Governments are now imposing controlled fishing zones and limits on the numbers of fish caught by fishing vessels *(above right)*, while large-scale aquaculture *(see page 25)* is another step towards a solution.

**ENDING EROSION**
Terraces *(see page 5)* are now being built in an effort to prevent the loss of precious nutrients from the soil *(left)*. In Africa, the spread of the desert is being restrained by networks of fences and new trees and plants, while walls are often built across valleys to stop the soil from being washed away.

26

# WATERING THE LAND

While the ancient system of ditches and canals *(right)* is still used in many areas, large-scale mechanical irrigation is now common on the world's bigger farms. Spinning water pipes can throw large jets of water over crops. Where water is scarce, drip irrigators give a carefully controlled supply of water to each individual plant, or pipes deliver a precise amount of water when required. In dry countries, such as Israel, large areas of land that were once barren have now become fertile thanks to careful irrigation.

### THOUGHTLESS FISHING
Huge trawl nets, used in large-scale sea fishing, can trap millions of fish at a time. But they also catch many other creatures, most of which cannot be eaten.

**THE MAYA** *This Central American civilisation flourished in the third to eighth centuries AD. However, from the ninth century onwards their civilisation declined rapidly and by AD 1000 it had disappeared completely. The reason for this is not clear, but the most likely explanation is that the Maya simply over-farmed their land as their population grew. This led to infertility of the soil and failure of their food crops on a massive scale.*

### THE DUST BOWL
During the late 1930s, 20 million hectares of land in the USA were ruined by a series of dust storms which destroyed crops. The storms were caused by poor farming practices. By turning vast areas of grassland over to growing wheat, the farmers did not protect the soil from the wind. The result was one of the worst ecological disasters ever seen.

# ORGANIC FARMS

Organic farming uses traditional methods to prevent pollution. Farmers plant different crops in the same field to keep the soil fertile *(right)*. They also use natural fertilisers, like manure and compost, and natural pesticides, such as planting onions among carrots to prevent carrot-fly.

### THE GIANTS OF IRRIGATION
In countries where water is plentiful, huge, moving crop sprayers are used *(below)*. They have soft tyres so that they do not damage the soil or crops, and they spray a thin film of water as they travel across the fields.

# THE FUTURE

The balance between the amount of food that is produced and the number of mouths to feed is reaching a crisis point. Despite the huge advances made in agriculture in recent years, farmers of the future will still have to grow more food and pay closer attention to environmental concerns. Because fertile farmland is now scarce, there is a growing demand for alternative techniques, such as hydroponics *(left)* and using space-saving frames *(right)*. The most up-to-date technology is also being used to improve crop yields.

WHO NEEDS SOIL, ANYWAY? Developed in the mid-nineteenth century, hydroponics is a method of growing plants without soil, either by placing their roots in water, nutrient solution, sand or gravel. The technique is useful for growing plants in places where the soil is scarce or of poor quality.

*Nutrient solution*

*Air supply*

THE BIGGEST VEGETABLES EVER! Developments in the breeding and cultivation of fruit and vegetables have led to the introduction of enormous varieties, such as pumpkins and cucumbers. Some of these plants even have inbred pesticides.

## OBSERVING THE EARTH

In July 1972, the satellite *Landsat 1* was launched. Its role was to photograph the Earth constantly *(above)* and send back information about the world's resources and how they are changing. This type of technology lets scientists foresee environmental problems. Action can then be taken to stop these or slow them down.

28

## SPACE-AGE FARMING?

*Biosphere 2*, built in the desert in Arizona, USA, is a sealed mini-world, with different environments ("biomes") – oceans, forests, grasslands, marshes and deserts. For two years, eight volunteers survived inside it, farming the land and living alongside 3,800 plant and animal species. The main aim of the project was to prove that life could be sustained there. This could lead to the development of space colonies which may be able to supply food to Earth.

*BIOSPHERE BIOMES*
Each biome contained a specific environment, such as an ocean, complete with coral reef, and grassland *(above)* with ants, termites and 45 species of grass.

## IMPORTANT ISSUES

A recent development in the history of farming is the importance of cruelty-free methods. More and more people protest against the mistreatment of animals on farms and in transport worldwide *(left)*, and many governments are now imposing tighter regulations regarding the treatment of animals and birds in agriculture.

### THE FOOD AND AGRICULTURE ORGANIZATION (FAO)

*This agency of the United Nations was established in 1945 to improve the world's farms and to raise the standard of living of poorer people. It provides advice and help, collects and distributes information and offers training. It remains, and will continue to be, an important weapon in the global fight against hunger.*

THE FAO

# GAZETTEER

**Aquaculture** Begun in China over 4,000 years ago; an alternative to fishing.

**Aztecs** A Mexican civilisation of the fifteenth and sixteenth centuries AD; destroyed by the Spaniards.

**Bananas** Banana plantations first sprang up in the 1860s.

**Beekeeping** Begun by Stone Age peoples, who used hives made of logs or pots.

**Breeding** Selective breeding has been practised for centuries. Breakthroughs were made after the 1700s. Today, scientists can control an organism's genes.

**Camels** Used for herding by 1500 BC. In Africa and Asia, they are used for farm work and for meat, milk and wool.

**Cattle** Bred over 9,000 years ago; herded by nomads. Oxen were used for farm work. There are many types, bred for specific needs.

**Cereals** A group of crops, including wheat, barley and maize, which are harvested to produce grain.

**Combine harvester** Developed from the combined reaper and thresher, combines were introduced in the early twentieth century.

**Cotton** First cultivated 5,000 years ago. The gin (1793) improved cultivation.

**Crop rotation** A Roman method of preserving the goodness of the soil by planting different crops at different times.

**Cultivation** Preparing the land for crop-growing.

**DDT** DichloroDiphenyl-Trichloroethane, first used as an insecticide in 1939. But it damages animals and crops.

**Drainage** A part of soil preparation, that takes water away from a field.

**Fertilisation** Developed over centuries. May be natural or chemical.

**Fruit growing** Early peoples cultivated wild fruit. Growers have now found ways of increasing productivity.

**Fuel** Natural products are farmed to provide fuel. Alcohol is made from sugar in Brazil and used to power cars; rape oil may also be used for fuel.

**Genetics** The study of how features are passed from one generation to another. Used to breed better animals and plants, it was developed in the 1800s.

**Grafting** Joining parts of two plants to produce one plant with desirable features.

**Grapes** Wild grapes were eaten by prehistoric peoples; they were cultivated for wine by at least 5000 BC.

**Greenhouse** A glass building for growing plants in which conditions are carefully controlled.

**Herding** Nomadic herders travel over thousands of kilometres to find food for their animals. Today, herds are kept mainly on farms or ranches, where farmers use motorbikes and even helicopters to round them up.

**Horses** Many species are bred for specific purposes – for example, Arabs were bred for speed and strength after AD 900. By this time, horses were also used for heavy farm work; this continued until the late nineteenth century, and still exists today.

**Hydroponics** Growing plants without soil; developed in the 1800s.

**Incas** A South American civilisation, destroyed by the Spaniards in 1532.

**Industrial Revolution** The period spanning the late eighteenth and early nineteenth centuries, which saw rapid developments in industry.

**Insects** Important foods in many countries; they might provide an alternative food source for many others.

**Intensive farming** As many animals or plants as possible are reared in the space available. But intensive animal farming is cruel and bad for the animals' health.

**Irrigation** Watering the fields. The ancient Egyptians developed the first efficient system; today, a variety of mechanical methods are also available.

**Llamas** Used for food, wool and transport in Central and South America; now farmed in other countries.

**Maize** A staple crop in many countries; first cultivated by Central and South American peoples.

**Maya** A Central American civilisation which flourished until the eighth century AD, after which over-farming contributed to its decline.

**Milking** Done by hand until the 1800s, when machines were invented. Cows are still hand-milked in many countries.

**Organic farming** A form of agriculture which uses only natural methods of cultivation.

**Ostriches** Farming began in the nineteenth century; it continues today for meat, leather and eggs.

**Oxen** The first animals used for heavy work on farms; replaced by horses after AD 900.

**Pesticides** Natural pesticides were used for centuries; chemical ones were invented in the late 1800s. But many are known to be harmful to people and animals.

**Pigs** Wild pigs existed 6 million years ago; bred since the Stone Age.

**Planting** Done by hand until seed drills were invented. Sowing machines are now pulled by tractors.

**Ploughing** Sticks were first used, followed by ploughs pulled by humans then animals. Now many farmers use cultivators.

**Potatoes** First grown by the Incas, potatoes were taken to Europe then worldwide by explorers.

**Poultry** Reared since ancient Egyptian times and bred by the Greeks and Romans. Poultry farming is still an important food source all over the world.

**Preservation** Natural methods have been used since ancient times. Today, chemicals and gamma rays are also used.

**Ranching** Stock farming on a huge scale, usually in areas of sparse grassland such as Australia and North America.

**Rape** Quickly becoming a major crop and the source of a variety of products.

**Reaping** Early tools were replaced by machines in many places after 1800.

**Rice** Wild rice was gathered in Southeast Asia thousands of years ago; it was farmed by 5000 BC.

**Rubber** First tapped by Native North American peoples. Many large plantations developed, but rubber is still tapped by hand.

**Shearing** Originally done with hand-held clippers; now mechanical.

**Sheep** Bred for 9,000 years; there are over 800 breeds.

**Silk** Secret for 2,000 years, silk production methods have not changed much.

**Slash and burn** An ancient method of ground use. Trees are burnt to make way for crops. Large-scale slash and burn farming can harm the environment.

**Stone Age** The era when people used stone tools, (2 million years ago-3000 BC).

**Sugar** Cane was grown over 8,000 years ago and spread worldwide; in 1799, beet was found to produce sugar.

**Tea** Its first known use was in China in AD 350; it is now grown on huge plantations, but the tender leaves are still picked by hand.

**Terracing** Cutting "steps" into hills so that precious nutrients do not drain away. This has been practised since ancient times; today it is becoming an important means of preventing soil erosion.

**Threshing** Separating grains from their stalks. This was done by hand until the invention of threshing machines in the 1780s; it is now done by a combine harvester.

**Tractors** Early types (1800s) were steam powered, followed by petrol engines. Modern ones run on diesel.

**United Nations** (UN) An organisation of over 160 countries, founded in 1945 to promote world peace. Its agencies include the FAO.

**Wind farms** A means of trapping the power of the wind and converting it into electricity, by using thousands of turbines (based on traditional windmills).

# INDEX

✶

## Picture Credits

# WINTER

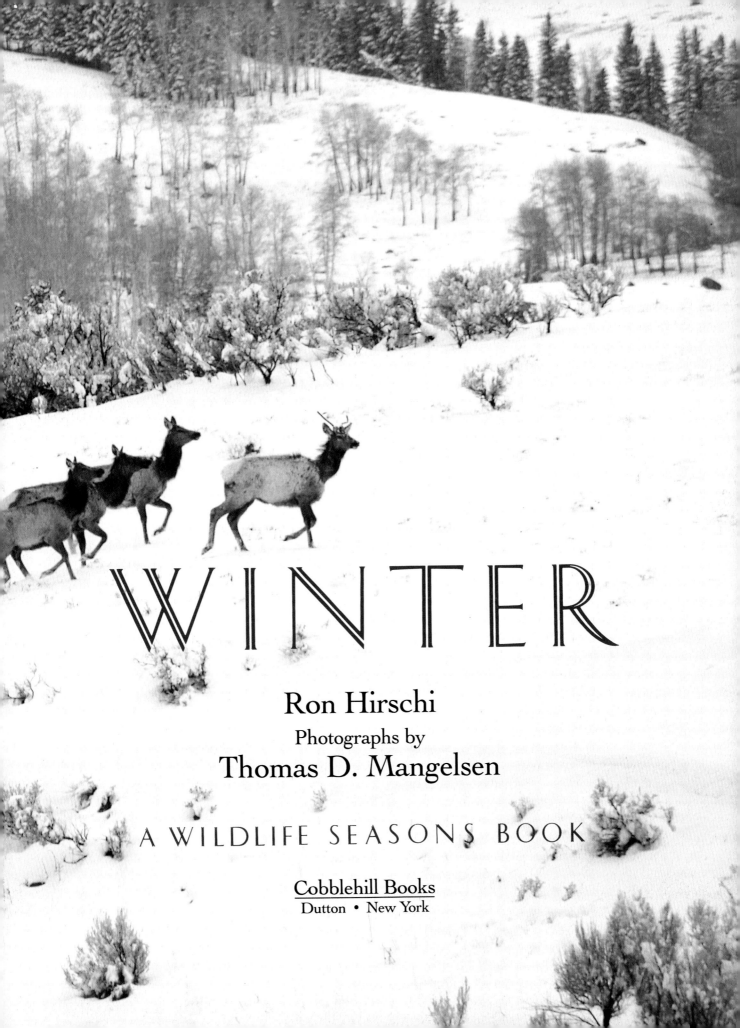

# WINTER

Ron Hirschi

Photographs by
Thomas D. Mangelsen

A WILDLIFE SEASONS BOOK

Cobblehill Books
Dutton • New York

**Library of Congress Cataloging-in-Publication Data**

Hirschi, Ron.
   Winter/Ron Hirschi; photographs by Thomas D. Mangelsen.
      p.   cm.
   Summary: Text and photographs introduce the natural world in
winter.
   ISBN 0-525-65026-1
   1. Winter — Juvenile literature. [1. Winter.] I. Mangelsen,
Thomas D., ill. II. Title.
QH81. H66 1990
574.5'43 — dc20                                                                                89-23935
                                                CIP
                                               AC

Published in the United States by Cobblehill Books,
an affiliate of Dutton Children's Books,
a division of Penguin Books USA Inc.
375 Hudson Street
New York, New York 10014

Designer: Charlotte Staub
Printed in Hong Kong    First Edition
10  9  8  7  6  5  4

*For Montana kids. You know best that*
*time when spring begins…    —R.H.*


*For my brother David  and his children,*
*Marla, David, and Matthew   — T.M.*

Winter is a hush of fallen snow,
a blush of rosy cheeks,
and a time for hot chocolate

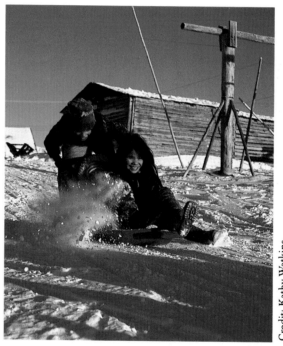

after the sleds
are put away.

But out beyond
the edge of town,
winter is weasel white,

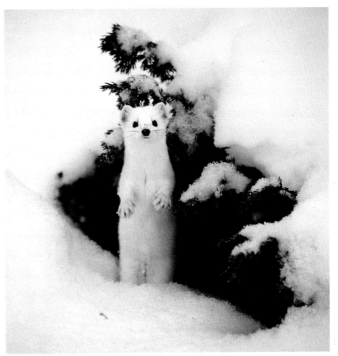

Long-tailed weasel

a dance of swimming swans,

Trumpeter swans

Dall sheep

and a time for
thick warm coats
on coyotes and
mountain sheep.

Coyote

Snowy owl

Northern pygmy owl

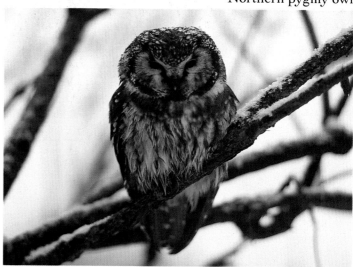
Great horned owl

W inter is
a season of
waiting owls.

Squirrel tracks

They watch
for mouse
tails twitching,
rabbits leaping,

Cottontail rabbit

Dark-eyed
junco

## and tiny birds

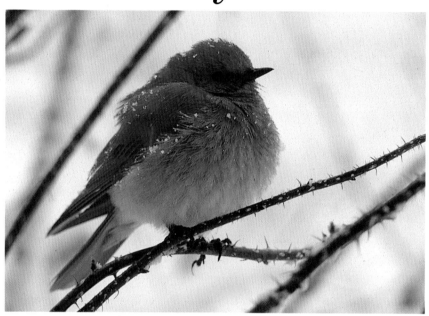

Mountain
bluebird

## fluffing each feather

Cardinal

Cedar waxwing

# to keep out the cold.

Winter is
an icy morning
when all is calm.
All is silent
beneath the deep snow,
inside the marmot's burrow,
and inside the bear's
snug den.

Mountain chickadee

Outside,
the icy branches glisten

while chickadees
search for beetles,
spiders, and caterpillars
that hide in
their cocoons.

Black-capped chickadee

This is the season
for ptarmigan
to hide in feathers
of white,

Willow ptarmigan

Canada geese

for deer to leap through
the crunching snow,
and for geese to wander
far to the south.

Mule deer

Robin

White-crowned sparrow

Winter is
a time for robins
and sparrows to
search for the last
summer berries,

for moose
to browse
the highest
green
branches.

Bull moose in velvet

And it is a season
that suddenly melts away.
Then springtime appears
like a sleepy bear waking
from its long, long
winter nap.

Grizzly bear

# AFTERWORD

Winter is not an easy time for plants and animals. Freezing weather and vanishing food supplies make life difficult. Some animals avoid this time of ice and snow in unusual ways; bears and marmots hibernate while many birds fly to the south.

Some animals are specially adapted to fit into the winter landscape. Weasels and ptarmigan change fur and feathers to a snow white each year, then shed their winter coats as spring approaches. Swans and many other birds have a dense layer of down feathers to insulate them from the cold. It is hard to imagine how, but tiny birds like the chickadee do keep from freezing their feet when snow blankets the ground.

Flight is probably the most wonderful adaptation to the extremes of winter, and each year thousands of birds migrate short and long distances. Many of these birds fly into backyards where we can have a welcome chance to spend time feeding and getting to know the wildlife of winter. A few sunflowers from summer will help the birds through the cold times. Their songs and bright feathers will offer you a little bit of spring, a chance to dream of the day when winter melts away.